SEVEN SISTERS OF OUR FAITH

By

Jane Short Hower

PublishAmerica
Baltimore

First printing

PublishAmerica has allowed this work to remain exactly as the author intended, verbatim, without editorial input.

ISBN: 1-60813-157-2
PUBLISHED BY PUBLISHAMERICA, LLLP
www.publishamerica.com
Baltimore

Printed in the United States of America

This book is dedicated to the memory of my parents,
Rachel and Samuel Short, who gave me the tools that
have guided my life: high ethical and moral standards and good books

Chapter One
Sarah

I am Sarah. I was once called "Sarai", but now am Sarah, which means "Princess". My name also means "The Mother of Nations". I became the first matriarch of what was to become the Jewish nation. This was the nation which produced such great royalty as King David and King Solomon. Sometimes, as you will see, however, my behavior was less than regal.

I was born about 4000 years ago in the city of Ur of the Chaldees, Babylon, in what is now southern Iraq, near the River Euphrates. This city was a center of culture and commerce because of its location at the northern tip of the Persian Gulf. Its craftsmen were surpassed only by those of Egypt. There were many wealthy families living there in beautiful tiled houses. My own family was very well-to-do and lived in what was considered luxury of the time.

My husband was Abraham, who was once called "Abram". God had changed his name, as he had mine, as a symbol of the covenant between us. Abraham was the son of Terah, who traced his ancestry back ten generations to Noah through his son Shem. That is why his descendants are called "Semites". Abraham was actually my half brother because Terah was also my father, but we had different mothers. This was not an unusual arrangement at that time. It was centuries before such relationships were prohibited by Mosaic law. Opportunities to marry were limited, so often we had to look within the close family circle for a partner. There was also the practical side of keeping property within the family

Abraham and I had a good marriage. My life became his life, not as a shadow, but as a strong influence. Together we experienced the hardships of nomadic life as well as spiritual blessings. My love and loyalty were rewarded by my husband's respect and devotion. There was, however, a dark shadow hanging over our marriage. At that time a woman was considered of little importance until she presented her husband with a son, for it was in his son that a man lived on. After some years into our marriage it began to seem that this was not going to happen to us. Abraham assured me that this in no way lessened his strong love for me, but I felt humiliated and the scorn of our community, and also my own sense of unworthiness.

Our tribe had many flocks of sheep and goats and herds of cattle. When the pasturage around Ur started to become scarce, Terah said that we would have to leave to seek better grazing for our animals. He took his sons, Nahor and Abraham and their wives, along with his grandson, Lot, son of Terah's dead son, Haran. We took all of our possessions, left the comforts of the only home we had ever known to become nomads for the rest of our lives.

Moving slowly across the land because of the animals, we covered only about fifteen miles a day. After many months we arrived at the walled city of Haran, 600 miles to the northwest, which is now part of southern Turkey. This prosperous city was a gathering point for trade caravans. We pitched our tents outside the city where we could pasture our animals, and remained in Haran for

many seasons. After Terah died there, Abraham, as his eldest son, assumed leadership of the tribe.

Eventually our people began to long for a land of their own.

It was then that the Lord commanded Abraham, "Go from your country...to the land I will show you. And I will make of you a great nation. I will bless those who bless you and him who curses you I will curse and by you all the families of the earth shall be blessed."

When we left Haran Abraham was 75 years old and I was 66. The possibility of becoming parents seemed ever more remote, but we had faith in God's promise. Not even knowing our destination we started slowly to the southwest toward the land promised to us by the Lord.

After we passed through Damascus we saw the hills of Canaan appear behind a ridge. At last we were on the frontier of the "Land of Purple", the Promised Land.

At Shechem the Lord appeared to Abraham and reaffirmed his original promise, "To your descendants I will give this land."

We made our way south to the old city of Bethel, which had been founded 100 years earlier. Here the Lord once more renewed his promise to Abraham.

When severe famine swept through Canaan we packed up our tents and headed south in search of food and water. Our wanderings took us into the fertile valley of the Nile in Egypt. In my younger days I was considered to be a great beauty. Now I was past my prime, but I was sufficiently well preserved to attract Pharaoh's attention. He wanted to add me to his harem. Since we had gone there seeking relief from famine, Abraham was afraid to deny his host. He instructed me to assent to the imperial advances out of fear of being killed on my account. To avoid falling victim to the custom that one could kill a foreigner to take his wife, Abraham told Pharaoh that I was his sister, but he forgot to mention that I was also his wife.

I chose to go along with my husband's wishes and I did not give the game away. I still shudder to think of what would have happened if God had not intervened to save me. Pharaoh's entire household was beset by plague. When Pharaoh discovered he that he had taken another man's wife, he sent me back to my husband with many gifts.

The years were passing by and Abraham and I were growing older. Prospects of having a son, let alone founding a nation, seemed ever more unlikely. Even though Abraham had received divine assurance that his descendants would be as numerous as the stars in the sky, the cradle remained empty.

Abraham's faith remained strong, but mine was beginning to wear a little thin. I really wanted to believe in God's promise, but it was so unreal to think that I would bear a child at my advanced age. I decided to take matters into my own hands.

If I could not bear a child for Abraham so that he could be Father of Nations, maybe I could get another woman to do it for me. I chose as my proxy Hagar, an Egyptian slave woman, who had been part of Pharaoh's gift package. What a mistake! The outcome was catastrophic! If only I had waited for God's plan.

Surrogate motherhood was an established practice in the world then. Just like today it was used by upscale infertile women who could afford to pay another woman to bear a child for her. Abraham did not protest.

After Hagar conceived she forgot my generosity and became upitity and proud. She lorded it over me.

I showed my jealous, but human, side when I complained to Abraham, "I gave you my maid and now she thinks she is more of a woman than I am. The Lord knows this is your fault, not mine."

Abraham did not act like a hero when he told me, "She's your slave. Do what you want to her", thus abandoning the woman.

With this encouragement I made Hagar's life so miserable that she temporarily ran away into the desert. There an angel appeared to her, telling her to return and prophesying an important future for the son she would bear.

Soon after Hagar returned to our camp she gave birth to Abraham's first son. He was called "Ishmael", but he was not the son of the promise. According to ancient custom he was to be considered my child, but I was never able to accept him.

About thirteen years later God spoke to Abraham again and renewed his promise of a son. This time it was too much even for Abraham.

He laughed and said, "This is a joke, right? Who ever heard of a 99 year old man and a 90 year old woman having a baby?"

Not long after that three strangers showed up at our camp. After we had offered them the hospitality of the desert I retired to inside the tent as befitted a woman. But I kept my ear cocked to hear what was going on outside.

When I heard one of the strangers say to Abraham, "Before another year is out your wife, Sarah, will have a new baby", I just could not help bursting out laughing out loud at this ludicrous idea.

The stranger heard me, came to the tent, opened the flap and rebuked me, asking, "Sarah, why did you laugh?"

"I did not laugh", I said.

"Yes, but you did laugh," he said. "But it will come to pass that you will bear a son in a year's time and his name shall be called 'Isaac', meaning 'Laughter'".

In fact I did give birth to a son just one year later, the little boy named "Laughter".

There is one last episode to relate, and it is not a pretty story. As the years went by my antagonism and resentment of Hagar and Ishmael became greater and greater. By the time Ishmael was a young teenager it had got to the point where I could not stand to have him and his mother around me. I could not even stand to look at them!

I went to Abraham and demanded that he send them away from our camp. I told him that I was afraid that after his death Ishmael would inherit equally with Isaac.

For once Abraham showed a little backbone and resisted. He said that it was just too distressing to think of losing his first-born son. Then God instructed Abraham to agree and to let them go. He said he would give to Ishmael the same protection he gave to Isaac.

Early the next morning, after loading down Hagar and Ishmael with provisions, Abraham stood at the tent and sadly watched the woman and his first-born son head out into the hostile desert.

They got along all right for a while, but when the provisions ran out and the water skins dried up Ishmael almost died. He was at the point of death when the Lord kept his promise. Hagar had closed her eyes because she could not bear to look upon her dying son. When God told her to open her eyes she saw a spring of fresh water. She gave her son a drink and he was revived.

Hagar and Ishmael learned to survive in the desert. She found a wife for him in Egypt and Ishmael became the ancestor of all the desert-dwelling Arabs in the Middle Eastern region. Isaac's descendants are all the Jews in the same area.

(The family conflict between Sarah and Hagar and their sons Isaac and Ishmael never ended. The struggle between their descendants continues to this day.)

I died about 1860 B.C. when I was 127 years old. I lived to see my son, Isaac, grow up, but I never knew his wife Rebekkah or their twin sons, Jacob and Esau, or Jacob's twelve sons who became the founders of the twelve tribes of Israel. At the time of my death we were still living as nomads, so Abraham did not own one foot of ground in the land to which the Lord had brought us. He had to purchase a field from a Hittite for 600 silver shekels for my burial spot. It was the only property Abraham ever owned in the Promised Land. His descendants would be posessors of the land. There the Cave of Machpelah became my final resting place.

The story of Sarah teaches us that God's ways are not our ways and that his promises are true.

Despite her less than admirable history both Jewish and Christian tradition have elevated Sarah to epic eminence. The author of the Letter to the Hebrews places Sarah's name among the great heroes of faith. So we could call her "Sarah, the faithful". But we know she could also be called "Sarah, the spiteful" and "Sarah, the scornful", as well as "Sarah, the human being" and "Sarah, the all-too-real person".

In her great desire to become a mother Sarah was driven to produce and protect offspring. The survival of the species and of the world depends upon this craving for motherhood.

Chapter Two
Rebekah

I am Rebekah. No one ever told me the meaning of my name. I knew that there were those who said it should be "Manipulator', because for as long as I can remember I have been able to get people to do what I wanted. I lived around 2000 B.C. in the time of Abraham. In fact I grew up in the place where Abraham was living when God called him to another land and made a Covenant with him. It was the city of Haran in Mesopotamia, now northern Syria. I had a very pleasant childhood growing up with my mother, Anna, my father, Bethuel, and my brother, Laban. You may think that since it was so long ago that we lived as barbarians. The truth is that we lived in a house made from reeds growing on the banks of the great River Euphrates, which ran right past our home. The men also used the reeds to construct boats which they sailed on the river to ply their trade.

I never thought we were really rich, but we always had plenty to eat and my father was able to give me some nice clothes. We had servants, but Laban and I were expected to work with them. Laban went with the men to hunt, gather food and care for the flocks. I worked with the women to prepare the food and tend our garden. One of our most important tasks was drawing water for the entire household, including our many animals. It was while I was performing this duty that my life changed forever.

I went to the well one evening with my pitcher on my shoulder to draw water. With the other women, old and young, I took the well-worn path to the watering place. We laughed and chatted as we waited our turn at the well. We were not aware that an old man, a stranger from far away, was lurking in the bushes with ten thirsty camels.

When he showed himself he said, "Let me, I pray, drink a little water from your pitcher."

I gladly gave him a drink, then said, "I will draw water for your camels, also, until they are done drinking".

It took quite a few trips to the well to carry enough water in my pitcher for ten thirsty camels. Before the man asked my name or inquired of my family he rewarded me with earrings, bracelets and a necklace, all of heavy gold.

Then he asked, "Whose daughter are you? Is there room in your father's house for us to lodge in?"

I replied, "I am Rebekah, daughter of Bethuel, son of Milcah, whom she bore to Nahor". Then I added, "We have both straw and provender enough and room to lodge in".

Then the man really stared at me with his mouth open. I did not know what was going on with him, so I started on ahead to tell my family that we were getting company.

Things started to happen really fast after that. By the time the travelers had arrived the food had been prepared. Before he would eat one bite the visitor insisted on telling us his name and his special mission.

"I am Eliezer," he said. "I have been sent here by my master, Abraham, from the Land of Canaan".

Then he explained that he faced the grave responsibility of finding a wife for his master's son, Isaac. Isaac was a special young man. God had told Abraham that he would establish an everlasting Covenant with Isaac and his descendants. Isaac's wife had to be a particular kind of woman. She could not be one of the pagan Canaanite women of Isaac's home country.

Eliezer said that this decision had weighed heavily on him, so he asked God to send him a sign so that he would make the right choice. The answer came that he should choose the maiden who volunteered to draw water for his camels.

I gasped! I had said that! I had passed the test without even knowing it.

Eliezer continued, "Imagine my surprise and delight to learn that Rebekah is the granddaughter of Nahor, Abraham's own brother. I am certain that she is the right choice. I respectfully request your permission to allow Rebekah to return with me to became the wife of Isaac".

Then he presented many gifts to my father and brother. The steward said he needed to know if they were open to his proposition before he could accept our hospitality. Bethuel and Laban practically fell over each other in their eagerness to give me to the representative of their rich relative. There I stood listening to everyone discuss my future and no one thought to ask my opinion.

The next morning Eliezer said that he was anxious to be on his way, with or without me. Laban and my mother tried to persuade him to delay for at least ten days, but he said he must leave at once. He had to give his report to his aging master who might die at any time.

Probably to stall for time my family finally asked me what I thought about all of this.

I guess I surprised everyone by responding, "I will go".

It was a little scary to think of leaving my family and everything I had ever known. I knew in my heart that I would never see any of them again. But I was excited, too, and filled with a sense of adventure. I felt that I was ready to leave my childhood and take my place in the world as a wife and a mother, a special mother of the son of the Covenant.

Now that it was decided, everyone flurried around to help me gather my things together. That same afternoon I mounted a camel and with my nurse, Deborah, and my maid, I began my long journey to another place and another life. My family followed our caravan for a short distance, then I turned and we waved our final farewells. I set my eyes on the road that led to a new life and never looked back.

We passed over the Lebanon highlands into the green hills of Galilee. Presently we drew near to the yellow plains around Beersheba. After we had traveled for many days and many miles we saw a tall man walking alone in a field. He looked up at the approaching caravan, shading his eyes with his hand.

I asked Eliezer, "Who is this tall man walking to meet us?"

"It is the master", he replied.

I immediately made my camel kneel, dismounted and pulled my veil to cover my face. Then I knelt, with my face touching the ground, before the man who was to become my husband, for this was indeed Isaac.

When we reached his camp, Isaac took me to his father's tent where Abraham greeted me warmly. Then Isaac took me to the tent of his dead mother, Sarah, a sacred place to him, and I became his wife. Isaac was forty years old and I was twenty.

What can I say about Isaac? He was a good man and treated me kindly. I knew that he loved me. I was so thankful that he never took another wife or concubines as other patriarchs did.

We had a happy life together, but there was a cloud covering our relationship, because as the years went by, we remained childless. Isaac prayed frequently and fervently to the Lord to send us a child.

After we had been married for twenty years his prayers were answered. God told me that I would become the mother not only of a child, but of twin boys. They would be different and never get along and contend with each other even before they were born. The sons would be two different nations.

"One will be stronger and the elder will serve the younger".

When the twins were born their differences were immediately evident. The first was very red and covered with hair even as a newborn. We called him "Esau", or "Red". The second had smooth skin and was born with one hand gripping the heel of his brother. He was named "Jacob", or "Grabber".

As our boys grew they went their separate ways. Esau became a boisterous outdoor person who spent his days hunting. He was the favorite of his father because Isaac loved to eat the wild game that Esau brought to him. Jacob was a quiet, thoughtful homebody who enjoyed the company of women and liked to cook, so he was my boy.

One day when Esau came in from hunting he was tired and hungry. He smelled the savory venison stew that Jacob was simmering on the fire.

Esau said, "Oh, that really smells good! Give me some of the stuff right now before I die of starvation."

Jacob decided to make Esau pay.

"I'll trade you the stew for your birthright", he said.

"My birthright!" cried Esau. "What good would my birthright be to me if I starved to death? Give me some of that stew right now!"

But Jacob was serious.

"Swear to me first!" he said.

Esau swore and sold his birthright for a bowl of stew. The birthright was the double portion of their father's wealth that should go to the eldest son.

There had been no deception, but it was not exactly fair for Jacob to take advantage of his brother like that. I did not have anything to do with this, but I was glad that my favorite son would receive the birthright.

As the years went by, Esau turned to the pagan culture of the area. When he was forty he married two local Hittite girls, Judith and Basemath. Isaac and I had disagreed on many things concerning our boys, but in the matter of our daughters-in-law we were in complete agreement. They were nothing but grief and trouble.

More years passed by. Now Isaac was almost 100 years old and completely blind. He knew that his days were numbered and he knew that it was time to give the blessing, the blessing that only Isaac could give.

He sent for Esau and told him, "Get your bow and arrows and go out and get some of that wild game I am so fond of. Cook it and bring it to me. After I eat maybe I will give you the blessing".

I was standing just outside Isaac's tent and heard all this. I knew there was no time to lose. As soon as Esau was out of sight I hunted up Jacob. I told him to get two young goats from our flock. "Bring them to me and I will fix them so they taste just like the wild game your father is so fond of. You can serve it to him and he will give you the blessing."

Jacob hesitated. He did not know if he should do this. Besides he already had the birthright; what did he need with the blessing? But I knew that the blessing was the most valuable gift my son could receive.

"Anyway, it will never work", he said. "As soon as my father touches my smooth skin he'll know I'm not Esau."

"Don't you worry" I told him. "I'll take care of that. You just go and get the goats."

While Jacob was out getting the goats I rummaged through Esau's things and found his best outfit. When Jacob returned I put it on him, covered his arms and neck with the hairy goat skins and handed him a platter of cooked meat.

Jacob took it to his father and pretended to be Esau. Isaac was surprised that Esau had returned so soon and he questioned if it really was Esau.

When he felt the hairy hands and neck he said, "You sound like Jacob but you feel like Esau".

After he ate, Isaac was still not convinced that this was his eldest son. "Come closer and let me kiss you", he said.

When Isaac felt the hairy skin, he said, "Ah, yes, this is my son Esau."

Thus Isaac bestowed on his younger son the patriarchal blessing which could never be revoked and which gave Jacob legal and spiritual power over his brother.

"May God give you of the dew of heaven,
and of the fatness of the earth
and plenty of grain and wine.
Let peoples serve you
and nations bow down before you.
Be lord over your brothers,
and may your mother's sons
bow down to you.
Cursed be everyone who curses you,
and blessed be everyone who
blesses you!"

Soon after Jacob departed from his father's tent Esau came in bearing his steaming dish. Isaac had to tell him that the blessing had already been spoken and could never be recalled. Then Isaac and Esau both realized that Jacob had deceived his father and stolen his brother's blessing.

I knew that it was wrong to deceive my husband like that and I did feel bad about it. At the same time I had always felt that God intended Jacob to be the son of the promise. How could it be that wild Esau with his heathenish ways? I was never one to sit back and let things happen.

From that time on Jacob's life was in great danger. One of the servants told me that she heard Esau say he was going to kill his cheating brother as soon as their father was gone. I knew I had to act quickly. I persuaded Isaac to send Jacob up north to my family so that my brother, Laban, could help Jacob to find a suitable wife. I reminded Isaac that we did not want Jacob to marry one of those Canaanites as his brother had done. Isaac consented and sent Jacob to my people.

Now in my old age, I was almost eighty years old, I was content in the knowledge that my favorite son was safe and in possession, not only of the birthright, but also the blessing. But it came with a heavy price. I never saw my beloved son again. The morning he left I stood at the gate and watched his departing figure grow smaller and finally disappear over the horizon.

After Jacob left home he deceived a few more people and at times he became the deceived. In time he developed a unique relationship with God, who renamed him "Israel". As Israel Jacob became the father of twelve sons, the founders of the twelve tribes of Israel. The fourth son, Judah, my grandson, was the ancestor of great King David and the greater Jesus, the Messiah.

Rebekah's story teaches us that some of the great people of our faith had many fault and imperfections, but that they could be changed and be used by God to form the foundation of our belief and carry out his work here on earth.

Chapter Three
Rachel

I am Rachel. My name means "Ewe", as in a female sheep. When my folks named me they must have known that I would become the shepherd of the family. I am the daughter of Adah and Laban, the son of Anna and Bethuel, whom Milcah bore to Nahor. We lived over 3000 years ago, just after the death of Abraham and into the last years of his son, Isaac.

With our other family member, my older sister, Leah, we lived in colorful tents just outside the city gates of Haran. Haran was a busy city at a junction point on the great caravan routes between the Mediterranean and Mesopotamia. It lay on a plain between the Tigris and Euphrates Rivers. (We are hearing about this area right now every day because it is now known as Iraq.)

As children Leah and I were taught the women's responsibility of caring for the tents. We pitched them, mended them and even made tents out of long strips of woven black, brown and reddish goat hair. Some of the tents were quite large and had curtains to separate the living areas. There was hardly any furniture. We made woven mats that were used as rugs, beds and seats.

I have to tell you that Leah and I never got along very well. There was always friction between us because everyone said I was the prettier one. I'm afraid I did not treat her very well, either. Leah was pretty plain and had something wrong with her eyes. She couldn't see very well and went around squinting. That certainly did not improve her appearance.

To keep us apart and because there were no boys in the family at that time, Leah and I were assigned different duties. She worked around the living compound and I was sent out with the sheep.

Late one afternoon when I took my flock for water I had a life-changing experience. As I made my slow approach to the well on the low-lying hillside I saw a handsome young stranger talking to three of the other shepherds who were waiting with their sheep. The stranger had just asked them where he could find a man called Laban.

After they told him, the shepherds said, "Here comes his daughter, Rachel, with the sheep right now".

I learned that this stranger was my cousin, Jacob, son of Rebekah, my father, Laban's, sister. After Jacob had removed the heavy stone that covered the well he helped me to water my sheep, just as his mother, Rebekah, had given water to his grandfather Abraham's camels.

Then he told me his story. Jacob had been forced to flee from his home in the hill country of Palestine to escape from his twin brother, Esau, who had threatened to kill him. This was because, with the help of his mother, Jacob had deceived his father, Isaac, and cheated his brother out of his inheritance. When Rebekah heard that the life of her favorite son was in jeopardy she talked Isaac into letting him come up here to her people. Besides, Jacob's parents did not want him to marry any of the pagan Canaanite girls as his brother, Esau, had done.

Now Jacob was so weary after his journey of over 500 miles on foot, so homesick for his devoted mother and so happy to be with some of his family again that he was overcome with emotion. He kissed me and wept out loud. (This is the only scene in the Bible of a man kissing a woman.) Jacob came from a demonstrative people whose emotions ran deep and were openly expressed. His love for me began at that moment and never once wavered. When I ran to tell my father who had arrived, Laban greeted his nephew as one of the family and invited him to stay. Jacob could not have come at a better time. Since Laban had no sons at that time he needed a capable son-in-law who could eventually take over the family holdings.

Jacob quickly became attached to me and I to him. He lost no time in asking my father if he could marry me.

Laban said it would be all right, but then he said, "You know, Jacob, you come here with absolutely nothing, so how can you give riches to the bride's family?"

Jacob offered to pay with his labor. An agreement was made that Jacob could marry me after he worked for my father seven years. Jacob declared that the time seemed as but a few days because of his great love for me.

When the time for our marriage arrived confusion and complications arose. The problem was with Leah. Since she was so plain Laban knew that he would have difficulty in making a good marriage for her, especially if I, as the younger sister, married first. Laban played a dirty trick on Jacob.

At that time there was no formal marriage ceremony. Following the custom of the time, Laban, as father of the bride, dressed her in long robes, covered her head completely with heavy veils and led her to the bridegroom's tent, at night. Only a dimly lit lamp gave any light in Jacob's tent. He was thrilled that at last he had married his beloved Rachel.

The next morning he got a big surprise. When the veils were removed he discovered that he had not married Rachel, but had married Leah instead! Just as Jacob had deceived his father, so had Laban deceived Jacob. He was furious! He went right to Laban and demanded an explanation.

Laban just shrugged and said, "Well, Jacob, you should have known I couldn't let you marry Rachel until Leah was married. In our culture the eldest daughter must be married first."

This was true; however, it was not according to the agreement that had been made. My father calmly suggested that Jacob could marry me at the end of the week celebrating his marriage to Leah. "But," he said, "you will have to give me seven more years of labor to make it official".

You can just imagine what it was like for me to have to share my husband with my sister. I knew he loved me best, and she did, too. That could not have been easy for her, either, but she never complained. Anyway Leah had the consolation of having all the children. One right after the other she gave Jacob four sons, while I remained childless. It was torture for me to have to listen to Leah's babies coo and cry and to watch them learn to walk and talk. Besides, it was humiliating. Everyone knew that children came only as a blessing from God, so it was obvious that I was being punished. When I told Jacob that I wanted to die if he did not give me a child, he became angry. He told me it was my fault because I did not give devotion to Yahweh, his God.

Eventually I resorted to an old practice among our people, as Jacob's grandmother, Sarah, had done. I gave my maid, Bilpah, to Jacob and asked him to treat her like a wife. When Bilpah bore two sons to Jacob they were legally considered my children. That did help, but it was not the same as having my own babies. Not to be outdone, Leah gave her maid, Zilpah, to Jacob. Her two sons were added to Leah's collection.

At the end of Jacob's fourteen years of service he had one daughter, Dinah, and ten sons. Just as I was becoming desperate, the Lord remembered me and sent me a son, Jacob's eleventh. I called him "Joseph".

After Jacob had been part of Laban's household for twenty years, things were beginning to change. By this time Laban had sons and Jacob sensed their hostility because he had worked hard and had become quite prosperous. His relationship with Laban had deteriorated also. Now Jacob was becoming restless and filled with longing to see his homeland and his family once more.

One afternoon he sent for Leah and me to go out into the field where he was watching his sheep. He asked us how we would feel about going with him if he decided to return to Palestine. For once Leah and I completely agreed. We would not be unhappy to leave our father after the way he had treated us. He had practically sold us and had cheated Jacob several times.

When Laban gave him permission to leave Jacob did not fully trust him to keep his word. He waited till Laban and his sons went away for a few days to shear their sheep. Then in the dark of night Jacob gathered together his wives, children, servants, flocks and possessions and stole away.

We traveled southward, crossed the River Euphrates and headed for Canaan. But I had a secret. Unknown to Jacob I had stolen our family household gods. These were little clay images that belonged to the head of the family. I took them as a right of inheritance so that Jacob could legally claim to be Laban's heir.

We had been gone for three days before Laban learned of our departure. When he discovered that his idols were missing he was enraged. Quickly he formed a party of some of his relatives and they started out after us. On the seventh day they caught up with us at Gilead. When Laban accused him of the theft Jacob insisted that he was innocent. Laban was certain that someone in our group had taken his idols, so he conducted a thorough search.

"So Laban went into Jacob's tent, into the tent of the two maidservants and into Leah's tent. And he went out of Leah's tent and entered Rachel's tent".

There I sat upon a camel's saddle in which I had hidden the little images. I knew that my father suspected me of being the thief, so I had to think fast.

I remained seated and said, "Let not my lord be angry with me that I cannot rise before him, for the way of the women is upon me".

Laban bought it and called off the search. He still felt that his gods were around somethere but he knew he would never find them. He called off the search and decided to leave.

After he had calmed down Laban made a covenant of peace with Jacob. They erected a pillar and called it "Mizpah" which means "watchtower".

They set stones around it and each man said, "May the Lord watch between me and thee while we are absent from the other." Then Laban told Jacob, "If you ever ill-treat my daughters or take other wives besides them, I will never hear about it. Remember that God is witness between thee and me".

Then Laban and his people started back to their home in Haran. We continued our southward journey.

As we drew closer to Canaan Jacob became very apprehensive about his inevitable meeting with Esau. Would his brother still be so angry that he wanted to kill him and perhaps all of his people? "When Jacob looked up he saw Esau and four hundred men coming towards him".

Jacob quickly moved me and Joseph to the rear of the caravan where we would have more protection. He was concerned for my safety since I was once again with child.

Jacob's fears had been unwarranted, for Esau ran to meet him, embraced and kissed him and both men wept. I was really pleased that my husband and his brother had reconciled, but they never did become close.

Just outside Ephrath, which is now called Bethlehem, the first of my birth pangs came upon me. Somehow from the beginning I knew that things were not as they should be. As time passed and the pain increased in intensity I became certain that I would never live to raise this child. There in a cave, with great difficulty, I gave birth to my second son, Jacob's twelfth.

As I felt my life ebbing away I cried out with my last breath, "Call his name 'Benoni' for he is a child of my sorrow."

Then I breathed my last. Jacob changed the boy's name to "Benjamin", meaning "child of my happiness" and loved him dearly.

There on the outskirts of Bethlehem Jacob set a pillar upon my grave. (That marker is the oldest single memorial to a woman mentioned in the Bible and can still be seen to this very day by travelers who pass that way.) This was the final expression of Jacob's love for me which began at our first meeting and continued my whole life through.

As Jacob continued his journey he stopped at the cave of Machpelah to pay his respects to his grandfather Abraham who was buried there. In Mamre he visited his father, Isaac, one last time. Isaac died soon afterwards and was buried in the family tomb by his twin sons, Jacob and Esau, who then parted forever. Esau went to the east to found the nation of Edom. Jacob, now called Israel, took his twelve sons and his daughter to Palestine and it became the country of Israel.

Although my physical presence was not with him when he reached his final destination, Jacob kept his love for Rachel, for me, in his heart forever.

This story of an ancient family teaches us that families have always been composed of human beings, imperfect people who can deceive and cheat each other and be mean to each other; people who with God's help can forgive and be forgiven and can change to be used by God to carry out his eternal purpose.

Chapter Four
Miriam

I am Miriam. I can tell you the meaning of names of my family and many of my friends, but I will never tell what my name
"Miriam" means. That is because no one ever told me. I do know that later on "Miriam" evolved into "Mary", a popular name for girls.

I am the daughter of Amran and Jochebed. I am sure that you have heard of my younger brothers, Aaron and Moses. We are Israelites of the tribe of Levi, but we lived as slaves in Egypt about 1250B.C.

Our people had come from their home in Canaan about 400 years earlier during the time of our ancestor, Jacob. When there was a severe famine in Canaan, Jacob brought eleven of his sons, all of their families and Dinah, his only daughter to Egypt for food.

One of Jacob's sons, Joseph, had risen to great prominence in Egypt. His power was second only to that of Pharaoh himself. As a courtesy to Joseph his people were permitted to live in the choice area of Goshen where they could raise crops, graze their animals and worship Yahweh, their God. The Hebrews became fruitful and multiplied.

The passage of time brought many changes to Egypt. After Joseph died a different regime came to power. A new king arose who knew not Joseph. He chose to forget all the good things that Joseph had done for Egypt. The king enslaved all of the Hebrews and put them to hard labor under ruthless taskmasters, and still they multiplied.

As more time went by the king became concerned because the

Hebrews were multiplying so rapidly. He feared that they would some day become so numerous that they would rise up and rebel against their masters. The king sent for two Hebrew midwives, Shiprah and Puah. As a method of population control, he told them that when they assisted a Hebrew woman at a birthing, if the child born was a boy they should kill him immediately.

These two women, Shiprah and Puah, come down through history as great examples of courage. At a risk of their own lives they defied the king's orders and refused to kill the children of their people.

When the king heard that the Hebrew baby boys were not being killed, he called in the midwives again and asked for an explanation.

The women bowed their heads before Pharaoh and said, "The Hebrew women are tough. They are a lot stronger that Egyptian women and give birth before the midwife arrives."

Then Pharaoh became very aggressive. He commanded his soldiers to go throughout the Hebrew area, seize all the male infants and throw them into the waters of the Nile River!

It was during this terrible time that my little brother, Moses, was born. Our entire family suffered great anguish, knowing that our baby was doomed to be drowned in the Nile.

My folks were able to hide my brother for about three months. Then my mother came up with a brilliant idea. She made a little basket out of papyrus and waterproofed it with tar. Then she wrapped the baby in soft cloths, laid him in the basket and hid it among the reeds that grow along the banks of the Nile.

I was twelve years old at the time and I was given the responsibility of keeping an eye on the little lifeboat, at a discreet distance. One day I had a terrible fright. I saw a group of Egyptian women coming to the river to bathe. As they came closer I saw that one was the royal Egyptian princess, Pharaoh's daughter. The others were her attendants.

Just then baby Moses began to cry. The princess heard him. Then she saw the basket and told her maid to bring the child to her.

"This must be one of the Hebrew children," the princess said.

"Yes, your highness", said the maid. "It is a Hebrew child and I must remind you that it is your duty to throw him into the Nile as your father, the Pharaoh, has commanded."

My heart was in my throat. Was I going to have to watch my dear baby brother being killed and not be able to do anything to save him?

But, no, the princess took pity on the crying child. As she took him into her arms Moses stopped crying and looked up at her with a big baby smile.

"Oh, look at that", said the princess, "I don't care if this is a Hebrew child. I am going to take him back to the palace and adopt him as my own son."

Then I had an inspiration.

I came out of my hiding place, bowed before the princess and said, "Your highness, shall I go and get one of the Hebrew women to nurse the child?"

"Yes, go", she replied.

I went and got Moses' and my own mother, Jochebed. She came and got the baby and we took him back to our little reed hut where he lived with us three years .

Then he was returned to the princess, as had been agreed. Pharaoh's daughter adopted him, gave him an Egyptian name, Moses, and raised him as an Egyptian prince. Moses was taught the wisdom of Egypt. This was important to him when he later became Israel's leader. His mother, Jochebed, lived in the palace to care for him. She insured that he was given instruction concerning his Hebrew heritage and his Hebrew God. Even though Moses led a privileged life he never forgot that he was a Hebrew and he sympathized greatly with his people who were being treated so harshly.

One day as he was passing a construction site Moses saw an Egyptian overseer beating one of his Hebrew relatives with a leather whip. Moses became enraged. He looked to the right and to the left and all around. When he saw no one he grabbed the Egyptian, killed him and buried him in the sand. He was sure no one had seen him.

The next day as Moses was walking about he saw two Hebrew men fighting.

When he tried to stop them, one said, "What are you going to do, Moses, kill us like you did the Egyptian yesterday?"

Then Moses knew that he had been seen and that he had to leave Egypt immediately. Not even Pharaoh could protect a murderer.

Moses fled to Midian where he became a shepherd and married a Midianite woman, Zipporah.

Once when Moses took his flock to graze at Mt. Horeb, which is also called Mt. Sinai, the Lord spoke to him in a burning bush.

"Moses", said the Lord, "come no closer. Remove your sandals from off your feet for you are standing on holy ground. I am the Lord your God, the God of your father, the God of Abraham, Isaac and Jacob. I have heard my people cry out in their distress and I have come down to deliver them. I will bring them out of the Land of Egypt into a land flowing with milk and honey. I send you, Moses, to Pharaoh to tell him he must let my people go".

Moses returned to Egypt. After ten plagues, signs and wonders, Pharaoh agreed to allow the Hebrews to leave Egypt and go to their ancestral home in Canaan. But at the last minute he changed his mind.

We had made all preparations to leave, so that when the word came from Pharaoh we began our journey. We had not traveled far till we encountered an insurmountable obstacle. There before us lay a vast expanse of water. I loved and admired Moses, but I had to wonder how he expected us to cross over the wide Red Sea.

Then we looked behind us and saw a great cloud of dust in the distance, so we knew that the Egyptian chariots, horses and riders were pursuing us.

"Was it because there were no graves in Egypt that you have taken us away to die in the wilderness?" I cried.

But Moses took us down to the water's edge.

"Be not afraid. Stand firm and see the deliverance the Lord will accomplish for you."

As we looked upon the sea we noticed the waters were being tossed about wildly by the strong east wind that had arisen during the night. Then to our great amazement Moses raised his hand and the sea parted right down the middle. A great wall of water rose to the right and another wall to the other side. Now we were safe—but, no, as we looked back we saw that the Egyptians had entered the seabed. Surely we were doomed! Then we watched as God performed a great saving miracle.

First the heavy chariots and horses became mired in the muddy sea bottom. Then with a mighty roar the waters from the right and from the left came crashing down. The Egyptian horde was completely covered with water and they all drowned in the waters of the Red Sea. We all hurried over to the other side.

I was so elated at this mighty demonstration of power and care of our God that I was moved to take my tambourine and dance and sing in praise and thanksgiving to the great Lord who had saved us. At that moment I was recognized as a leader. All the other women took tambourines and joined me in dancing and singing.

"Sing unto the Lord, for he has triumphed gloriously!
The horse and the rider he has thrown into the sea!"

It was my finest moment.

Not long afterwards as we continued through the wilderness I had a spiritual fall. I became a victim of jealousy and spoke out against Moses. I felt that Aaron and I were being pushed into a secondary position and that we should be honored equally with Moses.

"Has the Lord spoken only through Moses? Has he not spoken through us also?" I asked.

After Moses' wife, Zipporah, died he married a Cushite (Ethiopian) woman. I was jealous of her because this heathen woman put herself above me. I know now that I should have told Moses privately that he was setting a bad example as a leader to marry a woman from an idolatrous country and that he should have chosen a wife from his own people.

My mistake was to criticize him publicly. This undermined Moses' authority. People began to grumble.

"We should have stayed in Egypt where we had food and water. Now we have nothing!" they cried.

Aaron was pretty easy-going, so I got him to criticize Moses, also.

One day God called the three of us into the Tent of Meeting where he spoke to us in a cloud. He rebuked me and Aaron strongly for talking behind Moses' back and for rebelling against his true and faithful servant.

When the confrontation ended I was left standing covered from head to toe with the dread disease, leprosy. Aaron was not punished, but he sympathized with me.

He cried out to Moses, "O, my Lord, do not punish us for being foolish and sinning".

Moses did not respond to Aaron, but he pleaded to God for me. "Heal her, O I beseech thee."

God did heal me, but not till after I had been quarantined for seven days. I was led to a tent away from the camp, given food and water and left alone for seven days. After I rejoined the community I tried very hard to control my jealousy and helped Moses when I could while staying in the background.

Neither Moses, Aaron nor I lived to see the Promised Land. I died in the Wilderness of Zin, just seventy miles from Hebron and was buried at Kadesh. It was a measure of my people's respect that they celebrated for thirty days.

Although I died in the wilderness I like to think that my cry of exultation, "Sing unto the Lord", the song that signified freedom for the newborn Israel, would never die. (The spirit of this, the first national anthem, lives on in the songs we sing even to the present.)

(Miriam is the first woman singer to be mentioned in the Bible. She is also the first woman who was a leader of any importance outside her household.)

Her story teaches us the harm we bring to ourselves and to others when we allow ourselves to be overcome with jealousy.

In spite of her serious mistake, Miriam's story has been preserved because she had an important place in the hearts of her countrymen.

Chapter Five
Naomi

I am Naomi. My name means "pleasant", but as you will see, this has not always been an accurate description of my life and consequently of my disposition. I lived in the Land of Israel during the time of the Judges, the twelfth century B.C.

I wore the customary clothing of the time. The tunic was the basic dress of everyone. Men's and children's tunics were short and colorful. Women's fell to the ground and were darker, more sober colors. A lot of dark blue was worn. A leather or cloth girdle bound the tunic to the waist. At the end of the day the girdle was loosened and we lay down to sleep in our tunic. There was no night clothing. An outer cloak was worn by those who could afford it. Men, women and children of a certain age all wore head coverings. Men wore the traditional Hebrew skull cap, but it had a wide turned-up band that made it look like a turban. Women wore veils for two reasons. One was for the sake of modesty. No respectable woman would appear in public bare-headed. The other reason was to give them some protection from the intense Palestinian sun.

Only those who could afford to wore simple sandals. The rest of us went bare-foot. Clothing was very expensive. Many people owned only what they were wearing.

Wealthy women, and some men, wore much gold and silver jewelry. Earrings, finger rings, bracelets, anklets, neck pendants and jeweled head bands were very popular. This class of women wore heavy green and black eye make up and oil-based color on fingernails and toenails.

Many years had passed since our ancestors had escaped from their bondage in the Land of Egypt, conquered and settled here in the Promised Land. We still had no central government, but were a loose federation of twelve tribes bound together by our common ancestry and devotion to Yahweh, the one true God, as people of the Covenant.

It was a precarious time for the ten tribes living in the North. They had to defend themselves not only against the native Canaanites who still occupied some of their walled cities, but also from invasions of the peoples to the east, the Ammonites and the Midianites.

But I lived in the South, in Bethlehem of Judah, with my husband, Elimelech, and our two fine sons, Chilion and Mahlon. We were not involved in the great wars of the North, but did constant battle with another enemy—the climate.

Our semi-arid land west of the Dead Sea could sustain us in normal times when rainfall was sufficient. We were able to live off the fields of barley and wheat, grape vineyards and groves of fig and olive trees. But when the rains ceased the crops withered and died and there was famine, widespread hunger and starvation.

It was during such a disastrous famine that Elimelech decided that we should leave our home and seek a better place for survival. I was really surprised, though, when he said we would go east to Moab. To this day I am still not sure why my husband chose Moab. Probably it was because it was known as a land of fertile plains and ample rainfall. He may have had some business acquaintances there. I knew nothing of my husband's business affairs.

It was not a very great geographic journey to Moab—only thirty or forty miles—but it was a very great spiritual journey. The Moabites and the Israelites had not got along for years. Furthermore, the Moabite people did not honor our God, but bowed down to the terrible Chemosh, who demanded child sacrifice. I had many misgivings about raising our sons in that pagan environment.

We packed our things and went east to Moab where we found a pleasant white-washed dwelling place with a little field where Elimelech could raise a crop. Our sons were now old enough and indeed eager to help their father with the crops. I was able to handle the household chores. I was prepared to settle down and live contently in Moab with my family for many years, but it was not to be. Soon without any warning sudden and terrible tragedy struck.

I had just placed the loaves of bread in the outdoor oven for baking one morning when I looked up and saw the men walking in from the field. A great fear seized my heart, for I knew they would never desert the field of ripened grain at this crucial time of harvest unless there had been a great crisis.

My fear increased as the men came closer, because I saw that they were all walking very slowly with downcast heads. Then I noticed that the men in the rear seemed to bearing a heavy burden. When they reached the place where I was standing the men stopped.

The foreman raised his head and said two word, "Oh, Naomi".

"What is it? What has happened?" I gasped.

For an answer the foreman turned to face the rear of the column. As my eyes followed his glance I then saw that the burden that the men were carrying was Elimelech, and that there was no life in him.

As my knees gave way beneath me and my head started to swim, my sons came forward and they and the men helped me to sink to the large boulder that stood just outside our door. When I could find my breath and my voice I asked them to tell me what had happened.

"Oh, Naomi, I am so sorry", the foreman continued. "As we were all rushing to bind the barley into sheaves, Elimelech suddenly collapsed and fell to the ground. We were all right there and went to him at once, but the life had already left his body. Naomi, we will stay and help your boys complete your harvest if you wish and give you all the help we can in the difficult days that lie ahead."

In this time of terrible shock and confusion I could only think what a blessing it was to have such good friends in a foreign land, far from my friends and family.

Chilion and Mahlon were able to carry on with the help of our hired hands and friends. We helped each other through our grief and worked hard to keep our place productive.

One day when they came into the house for their evening meal, I took a close look at my sons and realized that they were growing up, as sons will do. I knew that they would soon be thinking of getting married, and rightly so. I always wished for my sons the joy and happiness that their father and I had had. The problem was that there were no nice Jewish girls in Moab. That meant that my sons would have to choose wives from among the Moabite women, women who worshipped Chemosh. Would they turn my sons from the God of their fathers?

Up to this time we had been able to hold on to our faith, even in these surroundings. Then came a horrible thought—would their children, my grandchildren, become pagans? And the unthinkable—would they have to be sacrificed to that awful Moabite idol? This concerned me greatly but I knew there was nothing I could do except to put my trust in the Lord that it would all work out somehow.

Soon Chilion married Orpah and brought her home to live with us. Not long afterwards Mahlon and Ruth were married and she joined our household.

They were nice girls and treated me with respect. We all knew that it would serve no purpose to make an issue of our religious beliefs, so we avoided such references. In truth it was a relief to have help with the household tasks. I was fast approaching old age when my strength and abilities would soon begin to diminish. I was forty years old already. We settled into a routine and had a comfortable life for a time. Once again I expected this to be a long-lasting condition. Once again it was not to be.

Soon another great catastrophe came upon us, suddenly, and in double. On the very same day both of my dear sons fell over in the field, dead, just as their father had done before them.

Now here we were, Orpah, Ruth and I, three devastated widows, facing a very uncertain future.

In those days no woman could inherit property, but only keep it in trust to be turned over to a male relative who might come into her life in the future—a husband, sons, or even an uncle, nephew or a distant cousin. Without men to support us we were sure to become dependent upon the charity of others.

I had no relatives in Moab. I never expected to get married again and the possibility of having more sons simply did not exist. Since I was responsible for Orpah and Ruth I thought hard and long about our situation. As I tried to find a solution an idea began to take form in the back of my head.

Just about this time we had a visitor from my homeland. A man from Judah was passing through Moab. When he heard that one of his countrywomen was in Moab he stopped in at our place. He told us that the Lord was once again blessing Judah with rich harvests.

This news made me decide to carry out our plan. I called my daughters-in-law to me.

"Orpah, Ruth, you have been good daughters to me and wonderful wives for my sons, but the time has come for us to part. I have decided to return to Bethlehem to try to seek a male relative who might take me under his care. You must not come with me, for I do not know if I could protect you against abuse from those of my countrymen who are still hostile to Moabite women. You are both young and attractive enough to find other husbands, so you must return to your mothers' houses and your families can help you to find other husbands."

Both women clung to me and wept.

"Oh, no, dear Mother, do not ask us to leave you. We will never desert you."

But I was quite firm, and a little mean, and told them that it was their duty to obey me. Finally Orpah gave me one last embrace and with tears streaming down her face said a final farewell and turned to go to her family. I never held it against Orpah for turning back.

But Ruth, she was stubborn!

"Entreat me not to leave thee", she said, looking me straight in the eye, "or to keep from following after thee. For wither thou goest there will I go, where thou lodgest there will I lodge. Thy people shall be my people and thy God my God. Where thou diest there will I die and there will I be buried."

In the face of such wonderful loyalty I could make no further protests.

Sadly Ruth and I gathered together our meager belongings and we began our journey. It was pleasant to have a traveling companion as we left the rolling hills of Moab and continued northward to the southern tip of the River Jordan.

Near Jericho we forded the river and headed westward through the hot desolate wilderness of northern Judah. Presently we came to the grassy hills of central Judah.

On the evening of the fourth day my heart leapt within me as I beheld the little white-washed houses huddled together on the hillside reflecting the pink glow of the early twilight. For this was Bethlehem, my home.

As Ruth and I came near to the town we noticed two elderly women drawing their evening water from the well. When they looked up at the approaching strangers I recognized my cousins, Rachel and Elizabeth. As I spoke their names they showed no sign of recognition.

"Oh, my cousins, please tell me you have not forgotten me", I pled.

After an intense look at me Rachel said, "Is that really you, Naomi? It looks like you, but how you have changed!"

"Yes, it really is me and I have changed", I replied, "and do not call me 'Naomi', for I am no longer 'pleasant'. Call me 'Mara' because the Lord has dealt bitterly with me."

Then I told them of the troubles we had had in Moab and introduced them to Ruth.

The cousins helped Ruth and me to find affordable lodgings for the night. It was such a comfortable place that we decided to stay there. While we rested for a few days from our journey we discussed plans for our future. Opportunities for women were limited.

It was the harvest season and what we had been told was true. The fields were richly ripe with grain to be harvested. Ruth offered to be a gleaner, but I resisted the idea. By this time I had become quite fond of Ruth and had no wish to see her join the women who bent over all day long in the hot sun scooping up the grain which fell to the ground as the reapers went through the fields.

Once again Ruth displayed her stubbornness. One day she came to me and said that she had heard that Boaz, a rich relative of Elimelech, was harvesting his barley.

"Dear Mother," she said, I beg you to permit me to go into the field and glean among the ears after him in whose sight I shall find favor".

I had to admit that it would be very beneficial to us to find favor with a well-to-do kinsman who could give us protection, support and security. I, myself, was unable to do strenuous labor, so there did not seem to be much of a choice. Once more my resolve crumbled in the face of Ruth's determination. After I gave her my blessing I got really sneaky and gave her some strong hints about attracting Boaz.

Boaz did notice Ruth and admired her not only for her beauty, but also for her hard work. When he inquired about the new woman in his field he was told that this was Ruth, the Moabite woman, who had left her homeland and her people to come here to be with her mother-in-law, Naomi, the widow of Boaz' relative, Elimelech.

Boaz did what he could to make Ruth's work easier. He instructed his reapers to drop more grain than usual where Ruth was gleaning and to keep an eye on her in case some of the men bothered her. Boaz honored Ruth for her devotion to her mother-in-law.

Before long Ruth and Boaz formed a mutual attachment and in due time they were married.

This marked a turning point in my life. Ruth and Boaz treated me as part of their family and found a nice place for me to live out the rest of my life in security, rent free.

When they laid their baby son, Obed, upon my knees it was like he was my very own grandson. This baby boy grew up to be the father of Jesse, who was the father of David, Israel's greatest king.

I shall never forget my dear husband, Elimelech, and our wonderful sons, Chilion and Mahlon. I have had many hardships in my life, as we all have, but I have found peace and contentment in my late years. I am blessed to be living in the land of my fathers among my people who care for me and worship our God with me. Once again I can be "Naomi", pleasant.

As I come to this point in my life I have learned that the Lord cares for us even when we fail to completely trust him. I have learned that God moves in a mysterious way so that a Gentile, Ruth, the Moabite woman, would become the great-grandmother of King David. I am blessed to be included in the family that produced not only King David, but also the greatest King of all, the King of Kings, Jesus Christ the Messiah.

Chapter Six
Hannah

I am Hannah. My name means "Grace". I lived at a place called Ramah in the hill country of Ephraim. It was during the time of the Judges, about 1125 B.C. This was an unsettled period for Israel. Surrounding nations, especially the powerful Philistines, were oppressing us sorely. Since there was no central government the twelve tribes of Israel had to depend upon a series of local judges for protection. Our freedom lasted only as long as the judge was alive. On top of that, many of the judges, such as Samson, had fatal flaws. The tribes were bound together by our common ancestry and worship of Yahweh as people of the Covenant.

This was also a low point in the spiritual life of Israel. Many had lapsed from the high standards of morality and spirituality as set up by Moses.

My home environment left much to be desired, also. My husband, Elkanah, was a good but undistinguished priest. In those polygamous times he took another wife. Her name was Peninah and she gave him several children.

My tragedy was that I was childless. This made me a target of scorn and derision not only of Peninah, but of the entire community. In that society childlessness was a disgrace. A wife's chief role was to provide children.

I knew that my husband loved me and I loved him, but it just was not enough. I yearned to have a son. I believed with all my heart that only

God could create children and that only God could convert a woman into a mother.

In those days of spiritual apathy Elkanah remained faithful and devout. Every year he took his entire household to Shiloh to worship and to sacrifice at the tabernacle there. It was the highlight of our year. Shiloh had been a central place of worship for many years, ever since our ancestors had set up the Tent of Meeting there during the time of the Conquest of Canaan. It was where Eli and his sons, Phineas and Hophni, were priests of the Lord.

Each year Elkanah and I and the rest of the family saddled our donkeys and climbed the autumn-tinted hills to Shiloh. Soon these journeys started to become trying ones for me. As I saw parents and their children coming together I grieved all the more because I had no part in the coming generation.

When we arrived at Shiloh Elkanah went into the tabernacle to worship and to sacrifice. A sacrifice was a thank-offering which allowed the worshiper to eat the meat that was left over from the sacrifice. As Elkanah completed his sacrifice he distributed the remaining meat among his family members. He gave portions to Peninah and her sons and daughters, but he showed favoritism by giving me a double portion. This increased Peninah's resentment and jealousy of me and she ridiculed me and made fun of me all the more for having no children. Although this grieved my spirit greatly I tried my best to cause no outward conflict or seek revenge.

As time went on this annual pilgrimage was becoming more and more emotionally draining. It finally reached the point where I could bear it no longer. One year when we arrived at Shiloh I broke down. I began to weep and could not get stopped, and I was unable to eat one bite of food.

Elkanah always treated me kindly and tried to be supportive, but he just could not understand the depths of my feelings or enter into my despair.

"Hannah, why do you weep?" he asked, "and why do you not eat, and why are you grieved? Am I not better to you than ten sons?"

I did not respond but arose and went into the tabernacle to present myself to the Lord.

As I silently prayed I made this vow: "O Lord God of Hosts, if you will only look upon the misery of your servant, if you will remember me and give to your servant a male child I will set him before you as a Nazirite until his death. He shall drink neither wine nor intoxicants and no razor shall ever touch his head".

My son's long hair would be a sign that he was dedicated to the Lord.

As I continued to pray silently Eli, the priest, came into the tabernacle. When he saw my lips move but heard no sound he asked me if I was drunk!

"How long will you make a drunken spectacle of yourself?", he asked, "Put away your wine."

"Oh, no, my lord", I answered, "I have had no wine but am a woman deeply troubled and have been pouring out my soul to the Lord."

When Eli saw how serious I was he joined me in prayer.

Then he said, "Go in peace. The God of Israel grant the petition that you have made to him".

This quieted me and I returned to my family happy and relieved. The next morning I worshipped with Elkanah and prayed with him. I continued to pray many times after that, in good times and in bad.

We returned home to Ramah and in due season my prayers were answered. I did give birth to a son. I named him "Samuel" meaning "asked of the Lord".

After I explained about my vow to Elkanah he could have voided the vow, according to law, but my husband truly loved me and he allowed the vow to stand. I knew that I was blessed in having a husband who loved me that much and supported me even though he could never fully understand my emotions. He was willing to give me the freedom to follow my own heart even though that freedom cost him a son.

I tended the little Samuel and I bestowed on him all the love a mother has for her first-born. I cared for him entirely by myself and never left him with anyone else. I even declined a trip to Shiloh with Elkanah because my son had not yet been weaned.

Soon after Samuel was weaned I dressed him for his first journey to Shiloh, where I would leave him.

The atmosphere surrounding Shiloh was sometimes polluted. Eli was a good man and a good priest, but his sons, Phineas and Hophni, were defiling the tabernacle by committing immoral acts on the very doorstep. I had no fears for Samuel, though, because I had placed him in the hands of God.

Before I left Samuel with Eli at the tabernacle I prayed a triumphal prayer in which I sang my happiness and belief in God. I prayed for those who had stumbled, but had been girded with strength. I prayed for those who had been hungry, but had been fed. I also prayed for those who were barren, as I had been.

Loving him as I did, it was a real challenge to return home to Ramah without my son. I felt in my heart that is was the right thing to do. I saw myself as a steward of God's gift and knew that this was the best way for Samuel to achieve his potential as a servant of the Lord. I could have moved to Shiloh to be with Samuel day and night, but I stayed at home and did not sacrifice the good of Elkanah. I attended to my duties and responsibilities and had a full and happy life.

I was pleased to learn that my son was being taught even as a young child to serve in the tabernacle by performing menial tasks, such as lighting candles and running errands so that he could rise to a greater ministry of the Lord.

The boy Samuel did his work so well that Eli appointed him to wear the simple linen vest worn by priests, which was called an ephod. I made him a little coat out of blue fabric to wear under the ephod. As Samuel outgrew one coat each year, I made another one and took it to him on our annual visits. When Eli witnessed my devotion, he asked God to bless me. I subsequently had three more sons and two daughters, as well.

I never forgot my firstborn, Samuel, and was content and secure in the knowledge that he was growing in stature and in favor with God and people. I knew that the son whom I had lent to the Lord would become great.

While Samuel was still young he began to prophesy. Soon it was known throughout all of Israel, from Dan to Beersheba, that Samuel had been established as a prophet of the Lord.

As a grown man Samuel became a priest and also the last and one of the best of Israel's judges. He had the high honor of being chosen to anoint the first two kings of Israel, Saul and David.

My heart had been focused for so long on my desire for a son that nothing else had mattered. It was only when I surrendered the object of my desire that I was able to find true peace.

We can learn from Hannah. Sometimes this can happen to us. If we set our hearts on something we cannot have it can rob us of appreciating and enjoying the gifts God has given to us.

Chapter Seven
Abigail

I am Abigail. My name means "my father rejoices", so I guess my folks had a really big celebration when I was born. I was there, but I don't really remember too much about it. I lived in the Land of Israel about 1000 B.C.

My husband, Nabal, and I had a luxurious home in the region of Maon, close to the larger settlement of Carmel, west of the Dead Sea. It was mountainous sheep and goat country. Nabal was the richest man in the area because he owned 3000 sheep and 1000 goats.

Our beautiful house stood high on a grassy plateau looking down on desolate brown hills, a bare valley and dry watercourses.

I know that it is a wife's privilege and duty to honor her husband, and I did try, but I have to tell you that Nabal was not a nice person. Too many times he lived up to the meaning of his name, "fool". He was churlish and mean, especially when he was drunk, which seemed to be most of the time. He never hurt me physically, but he was not a pleasant man to live with.

You may be wondering why I married such a person. It was because I had no choice. While we were still young children our fathers arranged for us to be married after we grew up. This was a common practice in those days. Opportunities for young people to meet and become acquainted were limited. Often they never got very far away from their own household. Parents saw this as a way to ensure that their children would be provided for after their parents were gone. Usually it worked out very well, but when one of the partners proved to be hard to live with there had to be some adjustments made.

So now you are probably wondering why I didn't just leave after I found out what my husband was really like. That was never an option for several reasons.

First, there was no place for me to go. There was a system of divorce in place then, but a divorced woman had no standing in the society of that day. If she was a widow, the community would see that she was taken care of. A divorced woman was an outcast because, after all, it was her fault that the marriage had failed.

I could not return to my father because then he would have to refund the bride price that Nabal had paid for me. There was only one way for a divorced woman to support herself, and I did not want to go there.

I knew that there always had been and always will be other women with less than perfect marriages. I knew, also, that some women were trapped in truly abusive situations.

Nabal was generous with his riches. He gave me everything that I wanted for my personal use and whatever I needed to run his household. Early on I decided to try to make the best of the situation and use my time and energies in managing Nabal's large household and staying out of his way as much as possible.

For some time I had been hearing a lot about David—about how he slew the huge Philistine giant, Goliath, by throwing one little stone with his slingshot, about his ruddy good looks and prowess in battle and about his rift with King Saul.

David had been Saul's official court musician. He played his harp and sang for him when Saul was in his dark moods. As David was became well known and popular in the land Saul became very jealous of him.

After David's defeat of Goliath he became a national hero. People danced in the streets and made up songs about how David's greatness exceeded that of Saul. Saul was emotionally unbalanced anyway, and that pushed him over the edge. He tried to kill David, and he almost got it done, too.

One day as David was playing his harp and singing for him, Saul snapped! He seized his spear and threw it right at David. David ducked just in time and the spear became deeply embedded in the wall not six inches from David's head! He got out of there fast and sought refuge in the wilderness around Maon, so David was our close neighbor.

He and 600 other young men with him were living off the land and having the time of their lives. They took it upon themselves to protect and guard the flocks of the sheep owners in the area against thieves and marauders. As a result Nabal's sheep prospered.

When David heard that Nabal was shearing his sheep he thought it would be a good time to remind Nabal of his protection. It was traditional in those days for sheep owners to compensate anyone who had guarded their flocks or helped with the huge job of shearing all those sheep. It was not mandatory, but it was the ethical thing to do. It was similar to our custom of tipping in appreciation for good services. The time of shearing was a time of great celebration and feasting, like the farmers' time of harvest.

David sent ten of his young men to Nabal. They were to say that they came in peace and came in the name of David, the son of Jesse. Then they were to ask to be included in the festivities since they had worked with Nabal's men to care for his sheep. Nabal's shepherds supported their claim and said not one sheep had been lost. Then they waited.

Nabal was drunk as usual and he flew into a rage. "Who is this David?" he said, "Who is this son of Jesse? There are many young men running away from their masters these days. As far as I am concerned David is nothing but a renegade. If he thinks I am going to take food and provisions away from my people to support him and his gang he can just think again!"

David's men were shocked! They turned around and left right away. When they reported every word to David, he was furious.

"Strap on your swords!" he said.

He strapped on his sword and started out with 400 of his men to seek retribution against Nabal. 200 had been left behind to guard the camp.

I had been really busy overseeing the feeding and entertaining of our many guests who had come to help with the shearing. I did not know about any of this until one of our herdsmen came and told him how Nabal had railed at David's men. The worker praised the men for the way they had protected our flocks.

Then he said, "You know how cantankerous the master is. Now we are all going to be punished because he won't listen to reason."

I listened attentively and I agreed that a strong man like David would never let such an affront go unpunished.

"All right", I said, "Thank you for telling me. I will take care of it."

I wasted no time worrying about my husband's character. I knew that I had to risk danger in order to avoid the greater danger of having all of our people destroyed.

Without asking anyone's advice or telling Nabal I quietly went to work gathering together special foods to take to David and his men.

I supervised the baking and packing of 200 loaves of bread, had five sheep dressed and several wine skins filled. Then we took five measures of parched grain, 100 clusters of raisins and 200 cakes of figs. I had our people load everything on donkeys and told them to start out. I mounted my own little white donkey and followed.

As we rode down a steep mountain ravine we met David and his men coming toward us. As soon as I saw David I got off my donkey and bowed down before him, with my head touching the ground. I can't tell you how much courage that took because I knew that David and his men were on their way to kill our entire household, including me.

"Oh my Lord, let the blame be on me", I said. "May my lord pay no attention to that wicked man Nabal who is acting just like his name— a fool."

I reminded David that the Lord had always protected him from his enemies—from the Philistines, from Goliath and from King Saul. Then I told him that I knew he would not want on his conscience the burden of needless bloodshed or vengeance.

David listened to me, then replied, "Praise be to the Lord, the God of Israel, who has sent you here today to meet me. May you be blessed for keeping me from bloodshed this day."

Then he accepted my offerings and said, "Go home in peace. I have heard your words and grant your request".

It was late evening when we returned to Carmel. Nabal was

celebrating the completion of the shearing and was drunkenly presiding over a huge banquet. I waited till morning when he was sober to tell him what had happened. As soon as he heard the news Nabal's heart failed him. He fell down with a stroke. Ten days later he was dead.

When David heard that Nabal had died he sent servants asking me to marry him. I accepted and became David's third wife and eventually the mother of his second son, Kileah.

We can learn several lessons from Abigail's story. First that it is sometimes better to try to make the best of a difficult situation.

Second, that it is sometimes best to risk danger to avoid a greater danger.

Last, that it is always best to leave vengeance to God, for it is written, "Vengeance is mine, says the Lord."

Bibliography

Deen, Edith, All the Women of the Bible
Harper Brothers Publishing, New York, c1955.
Reader's Digest, Great People of the Bible and How They Lived.
Reader's Digest, Pleasantville, New York, c1974.
Richards, Sue Poorman, Women of the Bible,
Thomas Nelson, Nashville, Tennessee, c2003